AF585531

Typewriter Music

Also by David Malouf

POETRY

'Interiors' in *Four Poets*

Bicycle and Other Poems

Neighbours in a Thicket

Poems 1975–76

Wild Lemons

First Things Last

Poems 1959–89

FICTION

Johnno

An Imaginary Life

Fly Away Peter

Child's Play

Harland's Half Acre

Antipodes

The Great World

Remembering Babylon

The Conversations at Curlow Creek

Dream Stuff

Every Move You Make

NON-FICTION

12 *Edmondstone St*

A Spirit of Play: The Making of Australian Consciousness

(ABC Boyer Lecture series)

Made in England

THEATRE

Blood Relations

Baa Baa Black Sheep

Jane Eyre

Typewriter Music David Malouf

UQP

First published 2007 by University of Queensland Press
PO Box 6042, St Lucia, Queensland 4067 Australia

Reprinted 2007

www.uqp.uq.edu.au

Typeset in 11/14 pt Adobe Garamond by Post Pre-press Group, Brisbane
Printed in Australia by McPherson's Printing Group

Cataloguing in Publication Data
National Library of Australia

Malouf, David, 1934– .
Typewriter music.

ISBN 9780702236310.

I. Title.

A821.3

Contents

Revolving Days

That year I had nowhere to go, I fell in love – a mistake
of course, but it lasted and has lasted.
The old tug at the heart, the grace unasked for, urgencies
that boom under the pocket of a shirt. What I remember
is the colour of the shirts. I'd bought them
as an experiment in ways of seeing myself, hoping to catch
in a window as I passed what I was to be
in my new life as lover: one mint green, one
pink, the third, called Ivy League, tan
with darker stripes, my first button-down collar.

We never write. But sometimes, knotting my tie
at a mirror, one of those selves I had expected
steps into the room. In the next room you
are waiting (we have not yet taken back
the life we promised to pour into each other's mouths
forever and for ever) while I choose between
changes to surprise you.
Revolving days. My heart
in my mouth again, I'm writing this for you, wherever
you are, whoever is staring into your blue eyes. It is me,
I'm still here. No, don't worry, I won't appear out of
that old time to discomfort you. And no, at this
distance, I'm not holding my breath for a reply.

Out of Sight

Painting the walls yellow was one way
of arriving in Sydney. I did it
via Brisbane and Birkenhead in '68, and the walls of
that room, stoked like the sun, were for two years my Harbour view,
    their surrogate
hum, the way the light bounced off them
like water or water music more an extended
mood than a space to work in,
a place where I forgot
to be happy because I was.

Grace notes, promissory
glimpses. Could paradise
be a colour? Can
music, the smell of cooking
from someone else's kitchen, table
set and the guests assembled, lead us there?
Or oxygen? Or prayer? In the free time being
of grace notes a yellow
wall blooms, a full sail pumped with sunlight, the clamorous swell
and pour it is making for still out
of sight, out of earshot.

Moonflowers

Gone and not gone. Is this
garden the one
we walked in hand in hand
watching the moon
-flower at the gate

climb back into our lives
out of winter bones – decades
of round crimped candescent
origami satellite-dishes
all cocked towards Venus?

One garden opens
to let another through, the green
heart-shapes a new season holds
our hearts to like the old.
The moonflower lingers

in its fat scent. We move
in and in and out of
each other's warmed spaces –
there is
no single narrative.

And we like it that way,
if we like it at all, this
tender conceptual
blue net that holds, and holds us
so lightly against fall.

First Night

A high dry attic room under warped pine-shingles.
        In the crisp air a scent
of last month's pears in straw, sheets folded on their laundry smell
        of soap and sky, an ironing
    -board, its hoof-shaped scorchmarks the ghost
        of old stains and burning.
            We slept well
    and deep in that mountain cold. Our breath went
out, dense with our bodies' warmth, and found no less a welcome
    in that place than in others.
                                    It is always
            a high room we climb to. The pears
might be garden tools, the laundry hay, the ironing-board an angel
    disguised by birthday wrappings; the same
        breath goes out, not always visible,
to join them. And they always, with the humility of those
        who are just themselves, make room
            for us. As when
we first lay down among them and slept the sleep of the innocent
    on unsettled ground, the first night out of Eden.

Like Yesterday

Always longer ago than we remember:
the day you said goodbye, my first
glimpse of the contrapposto
cherub and honey-thief, knee tucked inward, sucking a
    finger
-tip, and all
the instant sweet of things
stickying his mouth with mute hosannas.

Paint still wet on the grass, on
the daisy, the day's eye;
a big fish wrangled
ashore, live muscle fighting
the light of a scaling-knife. Goodbye, you said,
now, *now*, and all
the brute world's sweetness floods the angel's mouth

with more than words, the world itself, dumb
sorrow of beginnings,
that now and all it led to:
my heart midair, still
thumping, a fish unsheathing
its lightning-flash, suspended
on a breath. Alive. Speechless. Hooked. Ecstatic.

Funeral Games

These contests celebrate
the body. We show it
naked before the gods,

foot, oiled hair, long-tendoned
lean thigh and torso:
we launch it against time,

against distance, the thwart of
opposing cord and sinew,
to remind ourselves what

it is our companions,
down there in the dark
and watching, have lost –

what we, for all that the gods
and the dewy hills this morning
love us, have to lose.

As It Comes

Morning gets into its stride
with clean straw flying
and mares' tails. Outer garments,
rinsed and wrung dry
of their yesterdays, take
to the sky, lighter than souls.

Midday arrives
and drinks, as I watch,
the shadow of a clocktower.
A dazzle and a dazzle of chalked stones.

The sun blinks in a glass.
In the blinking of an eye
it is dark. First to gather
are starlings in unquiet flocks.
Then, quietly, the stars.

Rain Poems

Roofs

Patter of rain on the roof,
its variable touch
in the same house on tiles
on tin, as if what stretched over our head
more than another roof
was another sky.

In childhood our verandah
sleepout. Beyond its lattice, leaf
-tap, a drip toccata on the elephant ears and staghorns
of a pocket rainforest. Later
the slop of English skies on a 'sunny attic'
in Putney.
                    We lie down
in the one dark, in sleep
unbounded.

Discontinuous music,
of days that move on, nights that do not;
the authentic note,
once struck, endlessly sounded.

Watertanks

Squat corrugated-iron
clouds lashed down
with ropes of Morning Glory, galvanised
angels filled with the sky's
outpourings. When we washed our hair

in last month's downpipe music
it sparked with the electric
thump of horizons. When
we turned a brass tap-spanner
galaxies dripped

from our fingertips, our mouths
were enlightened. We stumbled
barefoot back to bed,
our sleep a sky-annex
busting to break away

up there, out there, dream-walking
the boom towns, the waterless
kingdoms. Rain-maker,
bull-roarer, invader brimming
with tall tales, hunkered down on

its stumps, translating back
to breath and bloodbeat in us
sheer paean, magnificat:
the amplified ostinato
measures of earthed sky-music.

Typewriter Music

Hinged grasshopper legs kick
back. So
quick off the mark, so
spritely. They set
the mood, the mode, the call
to light-fingered highjinks.

A meadow dance
on the keyboard,
in breathless, out-of-bounds
take-offs into
flight and giddy joyflight without
stint. The fingerpads

have it. Brailling through
études of alphabets, their chirp and clatter
grass-choppers
the morning to soundbites,
each rifleshot hammerstroke another notch
in the silence.

Recalled

Dew-touched guy ropes tauten
in no wind but the sky's
rekindling, our pup tent
simmers with breath.
Beyond its flap

tea-tree disentangles
from fog, water-lilies
lift into light
on the plover's wing, a hand-fling
of topknots resettles.

We move towards waking,
break clear of the spell
whose moonlit skin contained us
sleeping, love-making,
into stretch, into flow again,

reincarnate, as shy
by day, the rare night creatures
we turned to in each other's
arms go padding
away in our blood.

Flights

I

Late hammering from the forge. The sparks go out
on a sigh, psalms and proverbs

from a Book no longer quoted. Steeples drop
their shadow on dry-stick yards the size of a pocket handkerchief

and the handkerchiefs are waving. We have given
our soul to these machines.

A darkness bowls uphill. Lost among grassblades
it dwindles. In a tide

of mint deep to the hocks two Clydesdales wheel
and gallop. They will be creatures

again; they prop, they roll their eyeballs up. All this
years gone, in the age of collar-studs

and backyard tanks, home baking. The dream
of a boy back in the '80s. A dream he'll break.

2 *The Spin*
Amberley 1951

A light plane loop-the-looping
over sallow hills, all
its rivets snugged in

and singing; its beaten thin
quicksilver skin beaded
with cloud-lick, its hollow

spaces a brimful hum,
the pressure inside
and out in an equilibrium

true as the laws
of this world allow, a new
nature in the nerve-ends

reached or recovered, in
the shallows of the skull,
and the tilt, as they right themselves,

of road, fence, powerline,
horizon, a draft
of the way things are and were

to be, the long view still
breathtaking as earth
bumped in after the spin.

3

Metal cloud. I'll be home (meaning Brisbane)
five minutes before I've left, that's in no time

at all. Back in the eighties, back in nine-
teenth century cane and hoop-pine country, steam

heat, storm-streaked venetians. (Given this form
the end is taken care of, and one advantage

of living in an eclectic age is freedom
to choose, T-jet, a fast-packed antique vehicle hedge

-hopping towards that greener
state, that greener time zone, the near future.)

Our bodies are breakable. They break
all bounds and still arrive at their true nature.

I'm home. I've barely left. Just time to honour
forms, draw loved ones in (a line that holds) and
        I'm on the tarmac.

Millennium

1

The fire that starts in a dusty text in one part of the globe
is a shoe that flies to pieces in another

The angel's song caught like a wishbone in our throat

Unspooled and spilling
in the dark, quicksilver jump-cuts tilt and scurry

Hands folded in prayer

Wings of the metal dove that without preamble slides its
 thunder
into head after glassy head

2

Thinning stars
a residue of midnight
Days of disrepair

Seeking
as a stay to despair
the ordinary comfort

of loaves
and a rising

Like Our First Paintbox

Like our first paintbox: colour
in graduated rows more various even than the rainbow,
encouraging the eye
and the small adventurous hand to try for others, cloud
-castles of a sky more Disney-gaudy
than the azure overhead, as if mineral
dust and breath could reach alchemical midday
on a planet further off
than the one they taste and smell of. Bruise
violet and viridian a threat
of storms I could conduct with an index finger wet
from the cup, catching a hint of what God
felt, trying for this, then that; learning to see the earth
as it is from failed experiments – and even those we give
our hearts to and can't forget.
When sleep has unsealed
our eyes, we walk in the pink woods of that other world our hands
imagine – lost, like all
angels, in the flesh. Mauve grass, red weather,
the fruit gift-wrapped in its blue peel, O so edible!

'Poetry Makes Nothing Happen'

Silvery spellbound
trunks. Bark curled
and crisped like dry pork-crackling. Scooped
shadows in glazed snowdrifts. And these
deer knocking their antler-buds on wood, where do they
come in?
          The snowy spaces
of a page are their habitat, call up
trees and this nomad herd will find them.
Eye-pulp turned liquid
in a camera flash, they
startle. Trunks
vibrate to percussive thuds. The woods are barely
visible now
in the clouds they make, the pack of
their bodies, the meaty hot
smoke of their blood.
In our veins, slow-spreading
thunder. Unrecorded the lightning-stroke.

At the Ferry

A light as of axe-handles
swinging through fogbound scrub. Touch
wood. 'This is the last
time you will see all this. This is
the last thing you will see,'
the stranger at my side, no stranger, whispers.

I come with empty pockets
to the boatshed at the end of
the ramp, the river's breath stilled to a slow cloud beneath me.
And wait. And stand waiting.

Close by, either
behind or close ahead,
damped in the dampened air,
music. 'This is
the last thing you will hear,' the stranger
whispers. His last word.

I stand and listen.
Silence
approaches. A silence approaching music.

Reading Late at Campagnatico

A lighted room high up
among others at this hour
dark. My neighbours sleep,

so many windows
in a sky fogged with breath.
The traveller sees

from far off a light
hung low among clouds.
So close. Another planet.

It is the book
I'm lost in, as mind
swings loose on a fresher track,

and green as ever was
on this star, into
fields all folk, all creatures.

A concordance of such
breathy quick
ghosts sharing my watch.

Making

That a man should wonder
what he might find
at day's end beyond darkness,
something made
that was not there till he made it,

a thing unique
as all that our eyes
are schooled to: at its hour
at the masthead, Canopus,
a moon if it is writ

in the calendar, and this,
which Nature had not thought
to add but once
there cannot do without;
and whether of breath

made, or stone, egg-white,
earth, old sticks, odd clippings,
to be, as the child lost
in his own story seeks it,
a home, another home.

Seven Last Words of the Emperor Hadrian

Animula vagula blandula
hospes comesque corporis,
quae nunc abibis in loca,
pallidula, rigida, nudula,
nec, ut soles, dabis iocos?

1

Dear soul mate, little guest
and companion, what
shift will you make
now, out there
in the cold?
If this is a joke,
it is old, old.

2

Soul, small wandering one,
my lifelong companion,
where will you go
– numb, pale, undefended –
now the joke we shared is ended?

3

Little lightfoot
spirit, house
mate, bedfellow, where are you off
to now? Cat got
your tongue? Lost your shirt, caught
your death? Well, the last laugh
is on you. Is on us.

4

Sweet urchin, fly
-by-night, heart's guest, my
better half and solace,
you've really done it
this time. You've played one trick
too many. Fool, you've laughed us
both out of breath.

5

If this is one of your jokes,
my jack, my jack-in-the-box,
lay off. Where
have you got to?
It's cold out there.
And what will you do
without me, you sweet idiot? Go naked?
Homeless? Come back to bed.

6

What's this, old mouse, my secret
sharer? Gone
where? Did you think I'd let
you slip away without me after
a lifetime of happy scrapes? Who
warmed you, clothed you, fed you, paid with laughter
for your tricks, your japes? Is this the one
joke, poor jackanapes, dear bugaboo,
your emperor does not get?

7

So you're playing fast
and loose, are you? You've cut
the love knot. Well let's see how you get
on out there without me. Who's kidding
who? Without my body, its royal
breath and blood to warm you, my hands, my tongue
to prove to you what's real,
what's not, poor fool, you're nothing.
But O, without you, my sweet nothing,
I'm dust.

The Green Tavern

at five in the afternoon

For eight days I've been pounding my soles to shreds
on the flint of our northern roads. Get in at five
to Charleroi's Green Tavern; order bread with loads
of butter, ham warm from the pot, and feeling better
already, then great, stretch my legs out under the green
table and give an eye to the pretty pictures in
the wall-hangings. The waitress arrives, what a love,
with her big tits and her bright eyes, one
of those who wouldn't be fazed if you up and squeezed
her arse. With a laugh, sets down on its gaudy platter
my warm ham, pink and white, spiced with a clove
of garlic, my buttered rounds, and pours me a man-sized
Stella Artois in a long glass where the low
sun strikes gold each time I bend my elbow.

after Rimbaud

Goyesca

Witch's needle, a spark
smuggled into a haystack.

She's been sewing
dried toads, skin to skin,

a cloak against
the storm that's brewing

in a teacup in a neighbour's
kitchen. She's

nice when she's not
improving on the weather.

I've seen her with a frying pan
all smiles on her way to

an omelette, arms filled
with a grassfire of marigolds,

smoothing the sheet
on a hospital bed

as straight as any grave,
a pin slipped through her breast

pocket, where
that Witchfinder General,

the sun,
fingers it. Touchy

as cordite, she blazes
out. A haystack in flames,

a blackened cathedral
spire breaking the skyline.

A Second Ganymede

Don't you see what you're getting into,
Pyrrus? Snatch a lioncub
and before you can say
Gotcha! the wolf himself is on the run.

All claws, the lioness rakes
the surf pack for her toyboy. Is it
you, do you think,
who'll get him? Meanwhile, his lordship

idles apart, bare
-footed, damp curls dripping
on shoulders cooled by a kissing
breeze. Like that other

likely lad, the one
we're told an immortal updraught
caught napping at prick of noon, and sky
-jacked from the slopes of Ida.

after Horace

On the Road

On the road again, one fist in the hole I've poked
in a trouser pocket, my topcoat notional
as the sky I'm wrapped in, muse, your slave, your liege
lieutenant. Oh my! The affairs I've had a hand in
through that hole in my pants, Tom Thumb at his dopey
    dreamwork.
I'm up, I'm off again, I pop and scatter
rhymes. Shacked up at The Great Bear I'm knocked out
by the soft-shoe shuffle of stars, the late show. Back
to a milestone in the warm September dark, I take
the dew that wets my brow as a libation,
and ardour restored, great ghosts called up to cheer me,
I tug, elastic cord on cord, the strings
of that lyre my boot, my poor cracked boot, one foot
(some acrobat, eh?) set firmly on my heart.

after Rimbaud

Psalter

Beyond this page
swart robbers loomed at crossroads,
incendiary preachers
lit up a dark age,

moats hissed, a broadsword splintered.
All day fleeing
west, the names of farmsteads
burned in the head

of marauders. Their tongue
must hold out now in hill caves
among bracken, under
their breath a herdsman's song.

Rough words, but in them order
is made, mood
and tense reshape a story:
deep well, broad hearth, full larder,

field and faith well kept
in the rhyme, in the syntax,
a cup on high occasions
gravely unwrapped.

These runes make sense. A man
who cared for his trade
hacked them. Another
in a bad year took his pen

and held against mischance
this one pass: under
a sky blacked out
with gibbets, led the dance.

The Long View

Straw

To be spun out of gold
into gold. In summer fields
temples, pyramids,

in the swallow's bill mud-makings
of empire. A flute
for the god's mouth leading

bare feet down
from trampled light to chambers
centuries underground.

Weathers

The sun hangs on a twig
that in good time swells. From each
earth clod a view
of celestial continents
that throw down light, that throw down

rain, that throw down golden grain, largesse
of a land of too few souls;
what it can't use
it throws down, it showers
in plain gifts upon us.

Country

After dark in the dark
of our heads we shape it,
with thumb, spade-work, number.

Learn how a door swings open
where timber
creaks, off in the forest,

how pitchforks extend an arm.
A sulk of sunlit
glassy blue hills

in the milk a young wife pours.
Illimitable
light that strides in over

the sill.
Pushes
a chair back from the table.

A room without
walls, suddenly loud
with tales.

Anvil

This anvil a thundercloud
that smites black panes and cracks them.
Hammer: worn thin its handle,
head deafened with nails.

Among soot-stains and cobwebs, near
-at-hand angelic assistants
in all work go with us,
in all work are praised.

Struck steel, struck stars, of two
worlds the geometers.
On highways hooves, on the tooth-ridge
tongue-tap, formal speech.

Local Colour

The gods look down
on a slaughter-yard, walls
of ox-blood, roofs
of Jersey cowhide, nail
-rust, axe-murder colour. Hands
that deal in, think *red*.

For decades this
was all that stood between
us and the kiss of
snake-plains, wet rainbow
coils, warped views, the earth as devil
dance, all corrugations.

Even now you can feel
the blast it gives off
in the cool of night gardens,
the singe of hellfire
sermons, hot Sunday
dinners, dynamite.

Cities make shambles
of it, old shameful
beginnings, the squeal

of flesh tuned up to metal
pitch. A loose sheet rattles
whenever we're at risk.

Aftermath

Thorn soup, a bitter drop,
and the dream it brings a dream
of witches, of empty
shoes, glutted ditches.

Wet your mouth
with the small words that keep us
kin: the *thees*, the *thous*
of border exchanges.

From the Book of Whispers

Just between you
me and the

since even walls
more often than not

from this day forward
take heart and forget

remember only blood
is thicker

Nocturnal

A June night. Frosty stars
whirr above paddocks, breathless
treadle machines
in the pale grass hemming
sheets for a ghost dance.

Darkness creeps in under
a hedge. Its eye is on
the pullets, starlight sharp
in its jaw, blood
warm in the pullet's throat.

It is earlier than blood,
this landscape, and darker.
We make it,
we stare into
our heads to make it out.

Another landscape shakes
its dust from our bones.
Our bodies grow
lighter. They grow
light as we enter it.

Ombrone

Of trees their lucent shadow
on water, each leaf

remade, tumultuous drops
of light coalescing.

To be at once
in two minds and the crossing

made without breaking
borders, this

the one true baptism, flames
by water

undoused, and sound by silence,
each rinsed leaf stirred

by a giant's
breathing, deep underground.

Moment: Dutch Interior

Bronze-leaved
deciduous evening thickens
the window-glass, slow seconds

fall, a flicker
of particulate dust
in the room where a girl stands waiting.

In its slight imbalance
her body registers
the tilt of her heart towards

loss, some common sorrow not yet hers
but in
the world she has stepped into.

The specific
gravity of the moment.

The radiance with which
she fills it.

The absence
of another. Of others.

Thin as
a sliver of glass
a shriek from an animal-trap sprung in the grass.

Allemande

A peaceable silkshod army
at manoeuvres on parquetry.
The heart is a soft target.

Come home to the body
here, the giddy spirit
discovers the rules of play

more strictly than prayer
keep hand, foot, head, heart steady
and division at bay.

Swimming up out of a glassy
lake underfoot, ghost legions
of the dead they will one day

augment. In perfect cadence
a line reiterates
in the rippled melt and eddy

of a mirror the advance
in stately consonance
of its double, then, on a heel-point's

swivel, retreats.
Science has little to say
beyond cause and consequence

of heart or the heart's debits.
Art has its own bad habits.
The rest is history.

Mozart to da Ponte

Da Ponte, dear friend and collaborator, finder of words for me, this is the letter I shall never write and have always been addressing to you, my side of a conversation that has been in progress since we first began, always faintly to be heard under the music I found to fit your words, or rather, in the gap, which is not always silence, where words and music fail, and must always fail, to connect; in our case an attempt to move between Italy and our more sober North as if there were no Alps to cross.

It is a heavenly day – perfect October-in-Tuscany. I am alone (the others are off listening to Bach) and I have come back to thinking of the two languages and their impossible union, the compatible, incompatible marriage of two forms of experience that something in our very nature drives us to attempt, like marriage itself, but which is in the end no more than a gesture towards the reconciling of our divided selves, the one free and out of time in the eternal Now of being, the absolute presence of Here, the other conditional on time, place and a point in both which is the site of a story with a beginning, a middle and a foreseeable end; the one referring only to itself, the other forever looking off towards people, and a world of dizzying distractions: cats, clouds, cars, tears, opinions.

Words act, they get things going, they are sociable. They form unions, found cities, make contracts in which responsibilities are established and dues paid, or they break them and start wars. A sentence is a theatre in which something happens, it is all agents and events. But music is just itself. It has no story to tell, no truth to utter, and it cannot lie because it proclaims nothing but its own perfect presence. It is in that sense innocent, a form of discourse, like mathematics, that belongs to a time before we had learned to set ourselves apart by naming things or had found a name even for ourselves or one another. Music is the language of that state of grace we fell from and from which we never entirely fall. When it is so clearly at home, why should it want, as words do, to be elsewhere or yearn painfully, as words do, for before or after?

Children in the shadow
of a ruined keep are playing
Catch-as-catch-can
as breathless they plunge in
and out of history.
Air and sunlight swing
open. This is Today,
the Tomorrow that is Now.

They are solving an old puzzle.
Their cries catch at air
and miss, their bodies leap
and shadows start up
a growing fear; their own

small selves cast deeper
into time than Tonight even.
They waver, they fall.

But falling's a kind of grace
if they have it. Turning through air
and sunlight, catching as catch
can, they touch, they reach
their late selves, the leap
into space, towards Never
Will Be, the hope
made good and kept the promise.

They know they are breakable,
may fail, but must jump clear
across nine streams on the back
of a village plough-horse, work
their way through seven weekdays
a week till air and water
still and all journeys
end Here, where Now is all.

For music is free but may choose, and does choose, to incarnate itself and become human, as the gods in our older operas (and what are modern operas but the old ones in a new dress, with Jove in silk breeches and Semele a second housemaid?) descend from their timeless realm and a diet of ambrosia and nectar to sup broth at a peasant's hearth. The human and unfree, the realm of agues and intrigues, of joy, loss, sorrow – this too has its attractions, even for the all-powerful, the all-pure. It is the realm of chance and the gods are gamblers. It is the realm of change, which all changeless creatures long for, even unto death.

Music loves words as the gods love our world of unpredictable weather, as ideas, all spirit, long to be embodied in what is solid though breakable. It may be comic or tragic and is sometimes both in the same breath. That is what music comes down to when, putting off its divine abstraction, it embraces the actual. To have presided over that odd union, that marriage or liaison, may make us panders of a sort but it also makes us parents. Of that forced union, these works, necessarily and beautifully imperfect as they are, because entirely human, are the mortal-immortal offspring.

Yes, promise the clouds
like ragged children, *we*
are willing to come in
to the game, willing to play,
and *yes*, say the others,
lion, sword, stone,

we are willing to come out
and willing to abide
by the rules, slowly turning,

turning in a circle
in the charmed field, to be
as you wish, sunflower, tractor,

swan, teaspoon, bone,
or the three magic bullets.
But what will you give,
child, sitting alone
on a doorstep and solemnly
weeping, to have us

walk in out of
the rainy afternoon
and join you? Will you give us
breath? Will you call us
by our real names? Will you tell us,
in a whisper, your own?

You must have perceived, dear friend – how could you not have? – that that D Minor weather I conjured up for our *Don* was neither of the eighteenth century nor of Seville, and that it would demand some other action than the light-hearted entertainment your genius had hit upon. It struck a wrong note from the start. And when the mists cleared on an ascending scale, like the rising of a second and invisible curtain, you must have known immediately where we were. It is where we have always been; where I am now, call it heaven, hell or what you will. It is where all actions unfold and is as close as the breath in your mouth – I mean this world and the next in one. They are always one, which is why, dear friend, though Giovanni and the others may move through a jolly plot in one place, all avid for this and that as words make them, the victims of foolish dreams, wrong choices, an obsession with numbers and, in more than one case, a painful beating – mere whips to keep the play in motion – they have also, at the same time, to stand still in another and sing; a place where every action is already complete because it has nowhere to move to and no wish to move; and our ears have somehow to hear and accommodate both.

Your text was so witty, so irreverent, so human, so – *Italian*. Forgive me that in passing through my head (remember those rough Alps) it inevitably darkened. There was no terror in your *dramma giocoso*, it was all light and air. Not innocent, not in the least, since it belonged entirely to a fallen world, but it was in love with surface, with the lovely changing face of things, with what is presentable – with illusion; a dimension where, by a trick of the eye, the heavy cudgel stops just short of the back it is beating so that the victim's cries, our poor Masetto's, are purely formal, the little hell-flames that leap up are produced with mirrors, and the only Devil, or God either for that matter, is a benign but anxious stage-manager, whose one wish is to get through the performance without hitches and to send his audience home, after a few moments of vicarious alarm and a pretty tear or two, to their familiar beds, where no man is a Giovanni, though the dream may prod or threaten, and the Donnas Anna and Elvira have already settled for a carriage and a *cavaliere servente*. When you heard what my music had done, and became the first of my puzzled listeners, you shook your head, dear friend, nodding regretfully, and would have said, if there were not this old agreement of silence between us, 'Yes, yes, very moving, dear fellow – a masterpiece. But why this crack in the surface of things through which real smoke rises? Couldn't you have trusted the producer? They have machines for all that. Isn't the theatre good enough for you? Did you have, my little genius, to throw away every chance to *please*?

Ah, my friend, we belong to different worlds, you and I. It may be impossible but I wanted the thing to be real at every level. I had to pinch that silly Zerlina to prove that I was still awake, to make certain that the world was more than illusion. A nice little scream it was, all too human. It cut like a knife through that play world, even Giovanni was shocked; as if a more passionate lover, one of the gods out of an older opera, had cut in and stolen a march on him. It was me. It was my contribution to that other side of things that is *not* music, and not words either; which did not appear in the score and never could have; a grace note, but of a kind that precedes all civilised forms of expression, including music, and which I would like to believe that my Don really does leave room for. I wish I could be there at every performance to see that it goes well. To drive the singer up, as her flesh is caught between ghostly thumb and forefinger, to a pitch that expresses, in the most physical way, the pinch of the dark.

I had already felt it. The whole score was my extended

shriek, a *Requiem* can do no more. At that pitch neither words nor music can be discerned. It is the pitch at which most of the universe exists, but I had to lower it a little, tease it out, translate it back into what is accessible to our human ears. It was that, no doubt, that disturbed you and did not please.

Our audience out there, white-armed, bejewelled, plumply settled behind their feathers or regimentally frogged, do not care for bruises or real screams, however embedded they may be in sumptuous melody. That is for later; like the flames, if they exist. But the angel may be anywhere. We do what we can to translate his message into sound, and for those whose ears are attuned it is always audible at its own inhuman pitch. As in the pounding on an outer door. As in the dissonance that is created when three bands play at the same time and to different tempi. Or in a young girl's off-stage scream. Even the angel's announcement can be set to music and may sound well, as if what is given had been freely chosen after all and could not be otherwise. As indeed it cannot, though we close our ears at moments and refuse to listen.

Forgive me, friend, my deep betrayal, my feeling for the dark. That D Minor scale leads where I had not meant to take your too-engaging play creatures: into night and fog. I too have my passages of clear and bubbling sunlight, but there are pockets of D Minor where low mists gather that will not be dispersed – and no, theatre is not enough. There is also the pesthouse, the prison, the torture chamber, like the one they tell of deep in the rocks of the Festung, even at Salzburg under the leaping bells. Music must speak for some other, deeper action than the one your words embodied. And caught between the two, between the theatre, which is all play, and the pesthouse, the prison, the torture-chamber, your characters are lost and must sing more than they know, show us more than they appear to be, suffer more than even the most ingenious plot can arrange for them. In all of which they are, more than ever, alive and like us.

Swagged garlands, pear and orange
in stone baskets yearn
for a nature that's soft,
that *is*, and will change;

gilt columns support
a blue, neither Heaven
nor plain air, where urchins
with sideburns peep out,

use trumpet-call and bed-trick
to bully the fates,
and a sadsack's cuts and capers
can make the heart break.

Stage business: two worlds,
the fictive, the real,
approach, make a corner
but do not meet. Armed heralds

leap into the gap,
smoke swirls, swords clatter, words
that stroke, prick, lash,
crack corny jokes, call up

the dead to quick revivals,
find breath in a rag-tag
repertory where lovers'
discords, clamorous street brawls,

wars, end in the home key,
and fools, unotherworldly
-wise, play dead
to fight another day.

Pure make-believe, but played
out in the body
as events that are actual,
hot tears, raised hair, stopped blood.

And the players? Beyond pilaster
and candleflame they stare
back at the unruly
mob they stand in for,

in their mouths the dodger's wiles,
a mad king's bearlike howling,
one as our ears
and the gallery of angels

receive them. What we take home
is news of transformation
– our own, and a tune to whistle
in the dark of the tomb.

A Little Walking Tour of Southern Tuscany

The sun at a sword-stroke
leaps on to the scene.
Out of a cloudscape, rooftiles slick
with light, a rough-and-tumble
hill town tumbles
downhill, unravels its labyrinth at our feet.

What the world is
to travellers for whom
a quince tree, drowsy
sentry at the gate, recalls
to our lips the password 'coolness'.

A History Lesson

Sweaty after a bout the young prince towels his body,
sprawls against the wall of a tennis court. His body seems
his own. He is seventeen, loves exercise,
apples, and has just discovered order
in the frets of a guitar and the disorder
his spirit leans towards where hair sweeps upward
and a tender neck's laid bare. All this
is normal.

Miles away,
his body is the site of negotiations. Old men in furs
have laid it out between them, a treaty
is tied to the royal member as, by proxy, it is annexed with no compliance
on his part (it is, so far as he knows, off
in a goosegirl's placket) to the crib of a ten months' orphan, the Staatsholder
of nine dependencies.

Somewhere peasants
work in the prince's groin, sleep off the day's work in its shade.
They will speak the same patois when they go back
to dealing with horizons, but their heads
have passed under harsher laws. In a trench twelve pikemen
curse white, blow on a fist as night creeps over
the edge of a boy's body much like theirs and also forfeit.

These lives go other ways
than the documents intend. The young prince
will swell with evil fluids not drained off, his infanta
be occupied by three foreign husbands; she will never know his
  tongue.
One of that band of pikemen, every hair
on his head ablaze with firelight, every louse in his shirt assured of
its sweat, will get his wish. He will climb on out
of the blood of battle, eat, in a fiery sunset,
a late crust among shadows
that peck round a harvest blade, and whistling an old song, track
to its source among ferns the stream
that mutters in his head and never once says 'history'.

But that is another story. Passed from mouth
to mouth and not set down, it covers the facts, has a beginning and
  has survived
its middle. Why shouldn't it end well?

Madonna and Child with Goldfinch

Things are warming up. El Niño,
that cross Christ Child, is scowling up at Mother.
The goldfinch in his fist, having caught a hint
of 'changes', grows rebellious; the Child can feel it
wrangling in his grip, the tiny machine
at work behind its beak an angry alarm-clock
ticking. 'How did I get into this?' the Child
demands, 'or who got me
in?' 'You and the rest of us! Tough titty, kid,' his Mother
responds, but under her breath and keeps on smiling.

A curdled sea whelms red, shoals
of dead fish make its waters solid enough
to walk on. The earth is one. Pull
an apple from its bough and the whole garden
is touched. Growing unease like a new colour dis-
establishes the leaves, a change
of season, then each night the Weather News.
Which is not what we expected, what we believed
we'd walk in, hand in hand, when we took our first
gulp of helium blue and went trampolining up and over
the wall, on the broad path towards Gotham City.

An Essay on Angels – the short version

I

Have never seen one but being
curious am always
on the lookout, as I was
in childhood for white horses. Those

I did see, mostly
more than I had fingers
for, and though
expected, extraordinary.

Do I recall
the first, and having
before that none
to go by, how I knew it? Will I again?

Paddocks were empty
without, but rooms are not, and streets
are stocked, even over
-stocked with the imperfect, some

quite perfect enough.
The shock will come
later, when looking
back we see how struck

we were that things should be
so changed
and still
themselves, when we are not.

2

Restless. A haystack
of jubilant straws, muscle,
wingtip the fools

of flight. Restless. Eyelid
and nerve, all quick flame, curl,
ear-whorl, heel uplifted.

Stillness only
in the eye of this storm, as
subdued by gravity,

it weighs
the flesh and its surprises.
Attending on the world.

3

No tempting
them who are beyond
temptation with the scent
of herbs, old clothes, suitcases.

No calling
those who have no name
they'd wish to step back into.
They are past

all that, and that
is all we have: names,
hold-alls, smell and ghost smell
of where we were or would be.

Their gift is being
where they are. Waiting for breath
to release us, we fall
towards them. Idly

distracted, they turn away.
Then idly, on the hinge
of a second thought turn
back, and we are caught.

4

A preliminary
lightening, as of
air thinning out,
a room ballooning upwards.

We might need to be
at a certain altitude, even
at ground level, to bring
their heat into focus.

After that, all will be
just as it is
and should be. One,
half-kneeling to unlatch

his shoe, not even needing
to smile for you to get
the message, and no exchange
of names, just *This*

is for you, I think, and in
the hollow of his palm
nothing. The gift
we cannot reject.

5 *Unborn Angel*

The message in its mouth
a stalled breath. Bones in aspic,
wing-feathers still sticky
-moist in their sac.

Below, occasions
fail that should stir
to its calling:
famine in the ear

of corn no raindrop reaches,
a tyrant's heart
untouched, ditches
crammed with the meat

of born, unangelic
herds whose groans are bundled

skyward to stop the hole
that this one left unfilled.

Shit happens. Saturn rules.

6

Curled up like candied peel
in there
somewhere, and impish,
I've learned to live
with you and your nonesuch
notions and spills.

More carnal
even than I
at times can cope with, your
take on the angelic
leaves me
standing. A question

of balance? But somersaults
are not
my forte, or getting into

a pickle for the sheer
hell of it
my style of razzmatazz.

Une petite messe solennelle
your every
maladroit adventure,
heels kicked up
to magnify this
heaven you aspire to,

the flesh: its gravity,
its rapturous
assembly of smells,
the sadsack bag
of tricks you'll never get,
poor worm, to the end of.

A Veteran in the Field

Is the long truce off again,
Venus? Must there be
warfare between us?
At fifty I'm not the man
I was when Cinara held me
in thrall. Beloved
goddess, let this cup pass, tune
your ear to the prayers
of younger men. Take
Marcus – he's just your kind
of trouble if you like them
gamesome, athletic,
with a quick tongue and other
parts fit for the fray.
Let him carry
the day, or the night rather,
against some likelier jock
and he'll pay you
homage in the dark
with his funky sweat, the music
of twin souls panting
hymns in the mouth-to-mouth
style you prefer, in couples, boy
and girl, the dance

we dance, naked footsole
to hip, when we're not dancing.
I put no faith
in either, myself, girl
or boy, and I don't do parties.
Why then, why
Ligurinus, when I weep
so rarely, do fierce tears wet
my cheeks? Why
these stumblings – I'm a poet! –
into wordlessness? Why
these midnight encounters
when I hold you
in sleep, and when you slip
away in hot dreams stalk you
through room after room
at the gym, or in
the pool in breathless pursuit
down the fast lane of a golden
heel, back, shoulder that each
smooth stroke pitches further
and for ever out of reach?

after Horace

Raptors

Owl

The owl's eye, midnight,
total eclipse

for the fieldmouse stopped
dead where its shadow flares

on stubble. Thin bones under
the impact of the sky's

falling crack. The nightbird
hungers for what it holds,

all that is not
sky – groundwork, gleanings.

Since even owls do not end
in air, what they

hope to take in
is what these small lives know

of the afterlife, sunlight
ascending a straw,

the earth in close-up:
shock, then slow

aftershock collapsing
the horizons of a skull.

Kites

Elite black killer angels,
claws a confederate
close sect, high
rollers of sweep and harry.

A miracle unique
to mealtimes, the groundling's
blood-dream of flying
come true in their maw.

All else in the long view
waste, mere decoration
of lightpole and rooftile, fast
food heedless at play.

A hotline from brain
to hooded eye sorts out
the jigsaw components
of a landscape, what's

fixed, what merely stilled.
Baffled wingtips convert
the brunt of air to muscle
power, all wrestle

and pause, then suddenness,
breath passing
from mouth to mouth, quick snatches
of song. The imperative

dark consecration
of bane and being to what
comes once in a lifetime:
death, the flesh made flesh.

In the Field

At full point the sun. Straddling a fence-rail
in the rustling of spiked blades, I cast no shadow.

A breath, two bird-notes later, and it starts
away into the cooling field without me.

Towards

Piecing things together, meaning snowflakes,
to make this common light over the scene,

is possible, it must be, even in weather
whose dull skies won't quite make it and on pastures

too muddy real in a thick skull to be dazzled
with brilliance should it fall. We are children

in matters such as this. White, one colour
among many, and we've seen it, what more

do we need? The land lies open. Twig, tile, furrow
wait to be decorated. Let it fall.

It eddies over the sill and window-panes
are brighter for it; glad to reflect a morning

of one colour at last after so much turmoil,
red leaf, bruised cloud, the old glooms of a year

that rumbles to a close but will not end
the less, the more we're harried by; a thin

time for tramps and angels and Christmas coming
as ever was. The wet hills are littered

with shapes we cannot fit to the known shadow
of any leaf or bird, schoolrooms hum

with sounds that fit no music nor the syntax
of any local speech. It is not good

news, not by any road, that's coming to us,
old-timers croon. But snow falls, a change

and welcome. Those who believe will see it, having
opened in their mind a way for snow

to swarm out of the empty dark towards us,
transforming all we know, familiar paths,

familiar plots and proverbs to what we did
not know the land would bear: our footprints

approaching over the stilled earth towards us.
A stranger taps our shoulder, and we turn.

Into the Blue

Voyages

Jangling in my head the blue night-music
    of the Bay. Our limbs
emerged out of its salt.

When the moon blazed a track
    across it we were tempted. Only
our breath, only our need

for the next breath constrained us.
    It was our other selves
that tried it,

in sleep. And arrived
    safely. And never did
get back.

Stars

Its licking round our knees a shy demand
    for closeness. When we looked
    up, the sleepy stretch and dazzle of it
    took us
out and further out than thought could reach.

First apprehension
    of distance: the far, the near.
    When night came on
    in the wet sand instant
galaxies – look! – stamped out under our feet.

Rockpools

Glass you could put a fist through
    unbloodied. Red velvet
    mouths, skirts ruffled, claws, their sideways dart
and pause a stop start tango.

Distant rooms. When they fall still,
    in the underwater
    look that looks back at us the shock
of family likeness.

The Catch

Ribbons of drowned sunlight under the smoky
    flow. Boneless
    ghosts that flutter free of
our lists. They
    are the ones, the only ones
    we want on our lines.

Always the mystery of other
    flesh and occasions,
    creatures floating
clear of their future –
    us – and the slow
    ache of transformation.

Pinprick starry
    bubbles where feathers sprout.
    At six o'clock,
warm on a plate,
    the named ones, the catch.
    What we famish

for are the un-named
    others. Dropped lines trawl
    our veins for a colour –

blue, the blue of blue
    skies to collect
    our thoughts in as the first

planets clock in,
    and the Bay, that salt mouthful
    of the sea's unsounded
silence,
    yawns and takes up
    our story.

Afterword

After a whole day pressed
by crowds, the close, the loud
lives, some of them those
of loved ones or ones
nearly loved, the joy
of finding you here, embodied
silence I need not fill,

at ease after the roads
you've travelled and with just
a trace on your skin,
in the scent you give off, of what
you bring me, the light
you'll pour into my mouth
of fields where on the way

you rested. *But not*
tonight, you say,
not yet your smile assures me.
We are alone. No need between us
for speech. Take
your time. Eat the last
of the apple. Finish your wine.

Acknowledgments

Grateful acknowledgment is made to the editors of the following books and magazines in which these poems originally appeared: *The Australian Literary Review*, *The Best Australian Poems* 2003 (Black Inc.), *The Best Australian Poetry* 2004 (UQP), *Heat*, *Manoa*, *Southerly*, *The Sydney Morning Herald* and *World Literature Today*.

COMING IN 2008

NEW SELECTED POEMS
David Malouf

From the groundbreaking *Bicycle and Other Poems* to the superb *First Things Last*, David Malouf's *New Selected Poems* offers a resplendent, up-to-the-minute selection of poems by one of Australia's most distinguished poets. Malouf's best poems, with their grace, intensity and intelligence, remain among the finest examples of the Australian lyric. An essential compendium for all lovers of literature.

> 'David Malouf is arguably Australia's leading contemporary novelist. But this achievement has for too long overshadowed the fact that he is also one of our finest poets.'
>
> Philip Neilsen

> 'Malouf's voice blends erudition and music with masterful ease and acuity, allowing the worlds of thought, the body and dream to be integrated, and to flow forth with a sensual and transformative grace.'
>
> Michael Brennan

ISBN 978 0 7022 3635 8

UQP